LIVINGRY

LIVINGRY

A ledge(r)

GRACIE LEAVITT

NIGHTBOAT BOOKS
NEW YORK

ISBN: 978-1-937658-89-2

Design and typesetting by HR Hegnauer
Text set in Bodoni and Futura
Cover art: "Endless still life," an installation by Sarah Thibault.
    Photo documentation by Robert Herrick, 2012.

Cataloging-in-publication data is available from the Library of Congress

Nightboat Books
New York
www.nightboat.org

LA ROMPUE

Sparrows' special surgery
doubles at dawn, such
dubious rubber
burning azure up
to orange, which lunges
for patulous lungs, feelings
pulled in by their yarn
escort: the fiction
of this poetry is that
it all gets written down
by one person, ha, if I am
a broken woman
it is into
many, many pieces.

NONCE HEX FOR AND AGAINST INCISIONAL PAIN

Day plover-hued
like flaw secures
experience, snags
being how meaning
stacks, sticks along
a river catch
trash so each
sea copy (wave)
not caring to be
original cuts
into glamor, this
through me, light bent
with such sturdiness
of even a vegetable's
head, allium oddly
averaged against
the trillium. By turns
bilious and rebellious,
your whole
unpasteurized vial
(life) at once
a howling asset
when the Valium fails

to kiss as the body
starts to go
so we can
how brunette
sweethearts' wakefully
dawdle. Praise!
whose theater denies
exhaustion, my
exertion her
spiritual apartment, yet
sometimes it relieves
to let things run
out (together),
especially viral
whale-like feelings
that don't ever
seem to fit.

LOOSE LEAF

This morning
the mystery
shared itself, but I
don't want to
only ornamentally
absorb, therein
sly call perhaps
to be a part and
separate. It's possible
I pray for that
and not much else
these days, clobbered
into boots, bent
on seeking sanctuary
from our security
state. Vapors off
your orchard souse
me, reluctant
succulent, like
epic paperwork. Look,
we seem to rip apart
the world at
perforated edges, folds

where already it's holding
just barely together, plus
guess who struck
those first holes in
such neat, such
efficacious lines...
Meanwhile frankly
bodes the crocus' crotch
of one fur if
incomplete flesh—all
plantlife is
springtime's basic
confusion and the brusquer
queer in each
of us. Sometimes
I pretend I believe
not much in
waking, is waking
up, waking up isn't
much else, to enucleate
expectation and be
left with that
which toast, which
tisane almost certainly
can fulfill, really
any kind of water

put through
any kind of
leaves. So jug the stuff
or not, stack a million
tins or no, stockpile
fish pills, in any case
morningly we exercise (i.e.,
find some of us
still here) gathering
in the face almost
certainly of destruction
and I wouldn't want
to practice such
paper-thin, such
threadbare howbeit
embroidered arts with
any one but
every one
of you.

ALEX WHO SLITS HIS WRISTS IN THE BATH IN *THE BIG CHILL* ISN'T A PERSON AT ALL BUT COMMITMENT

I want to challenge myself
in the tournament of time
in which we find
ourselves painted
with description not only
to find nothing sacred
about smashing ants'
small bodies as they glisten
quick along the edge
of the tub I am in
as much as our tournament
no matter how hard
I commit their souls
to the bathwaters or purify
them in the flames
of so many clean-burning
candles—not only
to this but also to let
myself be overrun
by something more
than the hectic lonesome.

NUMBLING

Glory there is
some worry in
but also in
worry—I have
seen it.

TEARDROP TRAILER

Anxiety a hoopla for naught
but the hierarchy
of "little" things
hitched, which
recruit to unrequite
where I need to go from
who I need to be—not
popular as a secret, not
espousing inexhaustibly
borrowed feeling. But I
don't want to kill
the Angel in
the House. I wish
no harm on any
woman, even
a slice. Instead I'll go
out there to live—anyway
a wedge of light
is the House in the Angel
and every other
kind of murdered her.

SEETHING IS A KIND OF KNOWING

My water glass
with its chemical
spots, the dog
with little ticks, all
your children with one
big cough, it seems
by now a few matters
should have figured
how to overlap
some way other
than by proxy
war, how about a lens
through which
it's stranger to see
all your children
die by chemicals,
big coughs, little
ticks—seething
is a kind of knowing
but not understanding
is a lie I tell myself.

CAPPED BROOD

In the dream we shared
floral shirts over
fever bones like
the dessert, living
or dead. Living
one thing doesn't
absolve you from
another. A mother
telling the bees about
her son when
there are none
could mean there is
no telling,
triangulating being
how I get sometimes
at anything.

BALMER

Midsyllable is
a bad but
understandable time
for bona fide
mediumship
to end. A crash
course in spring
and what comes
ne— Some things
stay curved, delicate
as heartbreak
but do only flowers
dry so much
and lookalike? He was
love and he was
everything
leading up to love.

COMPOTE

Herb of women
to whom adhesive
some egregious
coronation, what
qualifies as a mood
swing, even? It's
such a good book
about blank and such
a bad book about
everything else, it's such
a good movie
about blank and such
a bad movie about
everything else...
Dreamboat, fleetly
recursive, I cherish
how you express
envy in ellipse
and to the point
of penumbral
feeling, how common
privet undulates
to the point of desultory,

dealing rutilance
out. My slippery
rhythm a runty
percussive guess
that our radio fetish is
so we might imagine
no silence, imagine sporadic
cordate oral baubles
as basic corporate distress.
Wanton ruffle, is there
a deep having, however
much? Of course
this packaging's
nondegradable,
meant to keep
us separate. So let's
make sensitive work
a practical strewment:
rosemary in breeze,
lavender redolent
accomplice to the sauce
—to save the world
except the world.

NONCE HEX FOR RAMBUNCTIOUS PROGRESS

Moon juiced
of its please, ink
of its dose, I plan
to address clarity
that there
might be some
clarity in address
and what
better preparation
than this bitter dazzle
that the sun starts
from nothing
every day
through a few slats
to become such
complex gold.

RADICAL ANGEL

Because some habits
of hatred get together
again, adrift in
connotation, and faith
won't parse this
healthy stain of her
contention, oh, low
lark, even when
your teachings do not
cohere I am
grateful for them,
untidy as the rose
spills starry sugar
visible only to the bugs
who need it. Fill
your nose with a place
that is food, chaos
that is a hoax; if told
just once, lo
the pressure but finer
the mist will come.

EFFUSIVE CONSTRICTION

Cut the window
very small

else this heart
will jump

out, a frog
into your hands.

THINK: PIECES

Let's insist it's not
disordered to care
about what we care
about, the lyric
flakes of felicity
everywhere while
pronouns such
faulty valves for
that which gets
included—the power
of this grammar
a clot heavy with
everything it's stopped
from forthing.

NUT GRAF

Rhododendron flutters
publish April, typing
slowly our drunk
feelings out
from swampy sinus
to obscure belonging
with vestigial
esteem, whose nub
I carry along
and rub, butts
earth's commonest litter
still in contract
with fascination, which
higher than sympathy reels
how we thought
this all would end
up more like growing
into who we just had to be.

RADICULOPATHY OF SPIRIT

Substitution is a kind of going
missing: diligently
nebulize and it spreads
as the greenery propelled
withal, its tiny helmets on,
to follow several viable affections
that might translate back
into a person. The kiss
flowers champion up
some ridiculous hill
once she gives is mine
but not its draft. This drinks
like a rootlet
rutilatedly sunk
into elaborate liquids...
without which would anything
really glisten? The effort
spangles with repetition,
famous for each piece of trash
that coruscates
to victory's freaky clicks
upon an exuberant budget

of wind. So now my tonsil
fat with thistle, full of nectar
smarts where more
disastrous coffee goes.

DAZZLESHIP

It is a kindness
his shapely haircut
skillfully encloses, but bless
what leaks, bless
the leakers, a flood
of blessings, for hell
is certainty; certainty,
hell, adjacent to which
is rutilance and I
am splashed by this, that sparkle
an unending vine
of so crushingly mingled
sympathies—its leafage
dizzy as our day was
gauze says:
be wilder than
bewilderness, bear
everything the argot will.

ALBA

Day breaks, is broken
whenever we take
ourselves away
from each other,
which takes
all shapes of
course and courts
its own particular
host of birds—not
the robin, the wren,
not the thrush—who mutter
between talent
and confidence. Just now
I can hear it, the music
of not quite yet.

NONCE HEX FOR AGILE THEATER
(E.G., THE BLACK-CAPPED CHICKADEE)

Over and
over that
you are
you is
a song
it's OK
to want
to be
near more
than inhabit
this place
—its two
mating notes
a column
of never
have I
evers: nursed
the berries
cursive; claimed
our clutter
some repair;
borrowed my

mouth from
you to
take this
species
of risk,
an incredible
office really
at the heart
of the possible
where
the women are
not asked
to apologize less
but the men
more.

NONCE HEX OUTSIDE THE CUTTING GARDEN

Famulus sawed
into like
saguaro fruit,
I want you to
do everything
to me, I want you
to leave
some things
undone—
solfège mixed
with broken sleep,
fluently enough
we call this healing.

AMYGDALA MADRIGAL

Brilliant little sister friend
of faeries and of devils, slay
me and be my best
self under a humble salad
of sky and air where time is
panic's opposite and
beloved. In a beige bedroom
across from some buildable lots
our crystal commute is to know
the whole libretto with a kind
of musical fitness. Lifting
up on its own edges, she catches
that mirrored underneath.

CUSHION CUTS, MOVING BLANKETS

If I could catch
like sparks up to
the whole of
the earth, its fringe
might be replete, its
headquarters
might be that
disparity describes
the fountain, whose
spectacular oomph
gives flowers head
and blurs the rock
it splits, making
my little times
another costly expression
as the finches rank.

TO QUESTION THE RITES WE RELISH IS A POLISH

June wanes
into wine
how the bird
fills with sky
its own body
up a blue
sponge to make
sound. It does
both the sucking
and the songing
out, effortful
wooly such
uncoagulated
moments, reluctant
to relucence
and snared
by the music.
Your talent for
tight meter
like "freedom
of speech"
can be a trap
stretched wide
as the state
has reach.

NONCE HEX FOR BAGGAGE HAVING SHIFTED

They are the TSA
agents who most
frequently compliment
my old caper-colored
suitcase, zippered
on its side, intimate
as expectation
into weather's vintage
negligee, potent like her
flippancy with talent
my foibles invite. It takes
a lot to be someone
else but we manage
this, with ribbons
internally tied, always
arriving sequel and rife
as wild carrots above
which royal umbels
seem to fly.

PASSING THROUGH

If anything happens,
let's meet flying
into that hot pink
streak we watched
from the plane
a reliable
constabulary of clouds
eat up, plenty meal
on tenterhooks, all this
way burning
and then some
septal defect rippling
sky's cyan welcome
peplum. We far from
the only sentimental
imbrication, it's
those mirror-tight places
taut enough
they start us to spring.

BUCOLIC RUBBERNECKING

Cenotaphic as a sofa
with nearly a deer bed
impressed, obsession
is the double
that severs me
from myself
while enigmatic schedules
marshal a haymaker
of autumnal light
your heart ponders
like a lamb's
shaky head
to rhythms of bright
plants. In our
too bone-filled time,
let the rows
of which the details are
communal be
fur as corduroy,
unseen until,
how a berry bush
in humps is budged
to sparkle, this love

more hardy
for its unkempt
varietal.

STATICE STATUS

The physic garden
responds in
autobiography–fronds,
even when you
despond, your reliable
huddle, cautious
encompassment, which
ravishes, comes
out of me into me
how a stitch.

CATTYWAMPUS NOSEGAY

With lobelias' bloodless
surgery into dirt
and the morning gloss
like receipt paper
everything rubs off
(spring the music
for moving parts) there's
something in the air enough
to recall each freak
relevant waft together
as those days I suffer
faith and igneous talk
are the same blue tarps
scabbing change
for a condominium
kind of feeling, the commute
dull as
the pain is sharp.

CONSPICUOUS PANG

We may fix bedclothes
yet change itself
be coverlet, and mauve
our assignment: massive
treatment to bramble. Like
the water it purples
with patience, this
involves wolves
and what else
such matted reeds
release. What lollygags
will gurgle humbly
over particulars
mineral enough to distill
a quality of obsession
that only because it won't
let itself complete
is ample as where
these branches bulge
to bear newfangled
weight. Is it
a stressful lesson?
Some quiet toward

your center balks
at silence
into which
a happy shout
is living air.

SUCK RHYTHM

Just below the rind
a cafeteria kind
of grief. There
my mood completes
the broth. Swallowing
air together
with seawater is
one way of pronouncing
clearly it's elsewhere
we'll be arriving. But crisp
with gothic advice
affiliation roses
your stable fire
like a bruise
making a place for itself.

SWAY WITH THE TACTICAL, COXSWAIN

Swoon in our money is
a heat, honey, how loose
the fog over survival

stars smooth, we tried
not to be tired, it
did not work out, mackerel

sky, factual frill, rosy he filed
I am an extension of
how this happens in

the fast boat division: red
clay wind, iliac wine
your lilacs hoist

with insecure rush, blood-
bright and municipal
liquid shrinks definitional

mouth concupiscent,
umbilical to a florid
pall, am floored by this

fish bladder of friends,
skeptical, their little kicks
and rummage punctuate

rime, fragrant through
lettuce lace, I have been
a part of what it looks like when

mullein more than fire is
common, radiant the
features of our sizable child.

UNIVERSAL FLOWERING

Tree covered
in katydid, why did
you grow that way,
bulged as blocked
carotid? "Because
I had to," the first
notebook said
the last notebook
would say.

VADE MECUM

Midmorning's prestige
as if earth might add
something to space, a mess

of agates in my palm, all these
mineral lines in freelance fit
run into yours. Now that

is what I call a handbook
—no title: so little
we can do, we should do it.

MEMBERSHIP

The moody care
that was mint
was smart
to have its seizure
it is famous
to appreciate
where shadows fill
this subtle club
for olive trees
I am not
so sure we ought
or want or get
to be a part of
whose executive grace
outpaces tangles from
the architects—really
spume is home.

RELATIVE SHELTER

driving to Perryville after the tornado and learning about exoplanets

Making photographs
under trees
near a thrill
of a hill
fixed doily
with shade
all your hair
colors all
I can think
is on some
remote planet some
distant day
our sun lotions
could be made
up entirely
of sun or at least
meant to store it,
not stonewall
beams from
this sensitive
surface, rather

hold warmth in
chorus. Then one
whopper of hawk
slathers doily,
light crumbs
as bat cliques,
obscure wisps
whip sky
into air— We really
shouldn't say
those twisters
"touched down"
unless lives
are the fragile
inner feathers
we mean.

PRAIRIE REHAB

It's easy to hide
when one looks peeled
already. Night
a natural cancel
for this
some flicker
readmits chatty
as the crickets against
cracked brackets
thick with estival
arousal– Quick! Poison
to death we still
might be. When I
eat a vegetable,
I want to feel
its fifty gifts
to my obstacle heart
on a vine there is
no finish in.

NONCE HEX FOR NURSE LOG

Sleep a visiting voice
outside space
and time. There
the very best
gets kept, while I
fiddle worry
a moss-like thickness
the whole panicky
earth for someplace
otherward and you—
so many people,
deciduous, stained
together, but where
is what we've been
erasing.

SORORAL COROLLA

Sappho said *you be*
ardent and it was
the sigh of
evening's equipment
gone out, how cursive
and irrepressible
as eiderdown. Women
sigh like evening's
equipment—it's not
not a thing, a pothery
thing, I'm writing
but each word
keeps slipping
toward whose elegies
are an autobiography
for everything. The sigh is
evening's equipment.

GARDEN PATH

Is it the dyestuff
of alphabets that
decants *clamantis* into
clematis, *begonia*
into *vergüenza*, even
morning toward
its worse horse,
later. And when
moms read this
book about reviving
Ophelia, are they really
trying to get up
inside themselves.

NO LANDMARKS DUE TO SWELLING

Perfection a type
of gossip about
how else this might
have gone and every
season a hormonal
dossier I am
new to, uneven as
the navy observation
up from within
chamomile's custody,
where we sway
with misunderstanding.
All of that to say
this is none of it
easy, this is all of it
finishing shadows
with fire, absolutely
everything enjambed.

WICKED SMALL HOURS DRAG

The wisdom off
my edges,
a night in
sections like
fruit, flowers
as loud
as certain
as death
and spiritually
bodacious
together unfold
cooperation. I
write up to
and including
my friends; you say,
"like a witch be
available to grace."
It is some butter
a little heat makes
clear and useful.
It is our myrtle
in sheets, a fold-
happy sea, that
ongoing tizzy.

NOTES ON CAMPESTRAL

However remote
the report the night
never sleeps. Irritable
splendor does
this waiting
a cotton spreads
false weather in
secular knots
at the quiet heart
of quilted rushing.
You know, that tune
of a candle guttering.

PLUMBING

Grief to which
time umbilical,
a kind of pipe-
dreaming titrated
to abyssal relief,
forthcoming as
a fountain—
through this
it's clear
as consequence is
vigil, these bones
might undertake
to turn
our attention
a deep-sea cream.

BIG MASCARA

Congratulations, oil,
every day you stay free
flowing underground,
the pearl appeal of which
its own education and
irreducible crucible I
trust is your desire, edgy
as the hour whose
appointment to a whole
century of lovers
an emptying scent
into this, our runty
acre, repairs, fixed
with grief to friable
earth, at fault—"you
and I fall together,
you and I sleep
alone"—the flinching
interns of how even
broken pieces ought
to pick up broken
pieces. Clayly we hip
into the kitchen, again up

in arms: Of course
a falconer knows
that power that bows
on return but also
—"all you're ever
losing"—the gutsy
gusty thrust of fucking
leaving off.

A VIABLE MAQUILLAGE

While even our wistful
ideas of solitude
away from us
are getting, lonely
as everything, in this mess
if emphasis the problem,
make your mark
portable as caffeinated
time is dedicated
to the cabbage moth,
which licks our neck
of night
school feeling,
there an agency
of cormorants
grinds its many chords
so moon and street
light mix into her
cheek their own
stray flower of being
always near to death
enough that one
move over might

bring down
its shaky bell. Let's pull
back privacy
from luxury
in the end.

CREAM RINSE

Watercolors acquaint
some service with gush
upon whose dossier
of bubbles, program of
swish I go: Meadow,
in your jumpy condition
you look pert as my fragile
pile of books, fleet as how
I fiddle worry
a moss-like thickness
the whole earth
with a head full of steam
about how strapped *affect* is
with meaning–*fake*
and *feeling*, both. It's unfair
but then at least we have
the lavender, all hues
of whales, whose aroma
in ebbs brings
an uneven comfort
to barrette back assumption.

IMPROMPTU BABY

Fragile fish
fall in his hair
inseparable
as air from my
amative comments
and finish where
unrolling means
not rolling around
the vibrant yeast
of your choice face.
Like sugar I hate
to prepare jealousy into
trim paper packets,
but it was pure
infatuation, down
to the minor antigens.

WELL-NESS

I'll have you know
each queasy daisy
some extreme memoir
about how whimsy too
will throw its weight, a clot
against this chemical
warfare, all kinds
being connected, against
this tiresome precision
of faces, against
the scallions' commodious
scansion. I want
to be wild
as the onion, whose
unmanaged readiness
produces tissues
in company with
absolute lusty thought—let it
become sentences, like silt
silk, more rhythm than
answer, for waiting
outside the tomb is
a diet more than one
time of year.

AUBADE

Summer's grief
a lucid choke

that bends that stave
as if advantage

some stove
which blends

all temps... lo
these different

pressures we ask
our people to be

a part of, snow
in the coffee,

trackless, coffee
in the snow.

CATENA

Routine sun shafts how
torn arroyo is bent
with greasewood, scant,
apterial, the scent. We

learn from exaggeration
through compact soil,
stipulate catena. "But, Jimmy,
he talks just as sweet as

you," pineapple weed rubbed
on your wrist, like mother's
uncle's ranch—not the worst
condition, outlinear season.

• • •

Other than skin, porphyry
story, proper dark among
friends, Sean's job is
Dan's cream door I

push a cushion against,
opening tender office
fruit. How docile to apply
away at subsequent lake, leaks

purple from the pressure,
miniature conservation
shifts... both times reading
this my partner fell asleep.

          •   •   •

Coddles fray through draw—
cellular rock, sprained, sweet
pea-pinned—mountain, how
abrupt a wine is porphyry, skin

of my lover is very wine until
ink until wine, ink, terminal as
rosette fattened upon rain, tawny
tenure of which lifts hulk up,

bubbleless about the sedge, infinite
pepper grass, demon within me
flashes, winter moon above water,
handles selvage. When it's over,

say, "the calligraphy was beautiful,"
"office fruit is a capsule," rocky bowls
dazzle far berm like your arm, warm
day sewn arterial to this loving cup.

●   ●   ●

for bpNichol

Deeper counting in a soil very
impossible to me, suspects
history, its sheer face. I want
to be talking strawberries

all of the time nipple-red with
language. Madness has many
uses not to be frozen, whole
list rushed to the head so you don't

sound like anybody over and
over: I was just being happy,
startling into relation things
one does not love but country

sun designs, asemic embolus
before elation, right up against
ruthless curation. Too many of us
die—there are too many of us.

• • •

Rechantingly alpine would I
compare how Jacob moves
with the moving sun Lee's
mountains out-gun, a song of

terrifying error. The sound
is absolute releaf. Sorry,
we can't have the party, gauze,
the cake, but a fresh thing, dull

thing, free flowers were one
road, roads, the whole way
there everyone working, kisses
piling, no churchy meal for

wan organizers up ahead
I've been disappointing, in
pink heat. Unimpervious ilk
requires waters, slower dancer.

Better the brief goal, early plum,
your sandwich in its paper package
—sharply was the storm flattened all
the berries, abolished the job.

• • •

Exhausted the essential lamp
regular friends of steel split up
in milliards words to sit beside
like grass blades. Her stubborn

frock suborns arterial sluice
chopped from sea, calico dark
with capillary action. Your art
eats love; my leaves are sex,

murdering associations, singing
evidence (insensible water loss,
thorough harmony, David dreamed
of you in a hurry, systole) yet we

flare into credentials, unequal lives,
best-practice poetry. Oh, innocent
alphabet, shimmering with your daytime
sense, skims Keston's communication

—energy to intelligence. The corn
has tassled up, our consideration
boiled over: in golden ribs a placeful
heart from otherwise ineluctable paint.

•   •   •

Splendor—more division where
a poem could have gone, I am
the muscle of an animal that lopes
felt through swale and an animal

that loafs, how star from star
differs, bones in our calendar
again, like formal summer Kate's
sexual grove ribbons together

young promise and the seldom
young, sloughs clumps of ribbon,
your attention, greening, drifts
to field dress the occasional

bursts to clarify his meaning. Course
it's granular material rests in angle
of repose, trifles pile up, we stop
doing anything at all, but long study

is great love, unsolved, sheepfold
outliving sheep, the pumping part
—starts more extreme air in
my hair than age affords.

• • •

NEEDLESS TO SAY

Where the track into grass
starts not to be one
but an accident
garden just this green
side of death
and how you break
into breathing inchmeal
is an apartment of happiness
that needles to say
no temple is simple
is how I ask myself
to faith. Sometimes I drink
to watch myself
have feelings, like about
how I know things. For instance,
the movie I'm watching
isn't over because
everyone they want
me to love is alive
and we have war movies anyway
since inside of a bottle
the inside of a bottle
makes sense. You drink

but you already know
—saying it over
and over again surely
is just this green
side of samizdat.

THE STICKS, WILILY

Like a student loosens
his paint to tighten
the intention, this
branch blown against
that derelict car
looks extra very
moving, if
embarrassed by its fledgling
assignment to unflinch.
Nota bene, self:
Growing pains. Do it
anyway. Work us
the way a blade does
light, scoring guarantee.

HORIZON CORAZÓN

Sun strips into
primavera plaid,
mixing patterns to
exuberant effect,
a sugar also
and eloquent. Her
hair flip sails
across my heart
and over everything
a viable maquillage
rhymes with everything
it covers to lubricate
collaboration. (There's
how we walk yet
hooves spark rock
in extra amounts.)

FIRE THE FALLOW, FARM THE MIRAGE

Curling often now he dandles
time, that rocky place
for our occupation I felt
innocent of, round eyes

far away, meatly nestled in
disappointment. Nostalgia
lichen-laced is delicious against
antique we lust; the mechanism

copes, pushes dirt toward
copse, road, till stars relent
new salt. Parched in field
office in fescue is perfect

venue for listening to Lou
Reed, Leonard Cohen,
chimeral kiss, milky tincture
of which equals archive

surviving fealty through
nakedhood, that is, friendship,
high, damp near the shadow
side of sumptuary... Hear

pneumothorax and think
butterflies. Hear the radio,
think medicine, laureate and
it's "Eugenio, please come

here so I can see"—spiritual
monocle through which
laurels absorb storm, springish
bromides, your dream, us

foxes feeding on strawberries
or feeding foxes strawberries
or feeding berries themselves
or just the colors, state by

state. What angel, impulse. Basket
case morning's plain arms wrap
around and wingéd to fool
the heart as void does past

compensation (concurrently
a nude notebook joy
and rage interannotate, moral
mystic embellished past

legibility—sugar, augur, ink, no
truck with endarkenment. Whereas
my soil hurts, blighted, united
in AUMF, now, therefore, be

it resolved: friends, competent
tribunals wanted). We don't give
enough, grieve enough, share
maybe pennies, very little

common gold... Oh, wild
raring, sweet evaporate who
crests whole, fruiting stalk,
my life is when observation

speeds to full, full sensing of
strawberries, hers, into violet
almost, amnesty, for hours not
spent awing our concentric

concentrations, juice at dawn,
forensic love, nakedhood.
Remember to take your sun
medicine, radio talisman, take

a walk when Hannah can't
cry. "It's just a flower made out
of clay... it's hard to live in
the city." But I'll paper these

walls however Jamie wants,
dapple whatever we can't
paper, play Lou, Leonard,
Erik, sit up in the dark

in orange wingback, perfect
venue for waiting. After all
we all are fruiting stalks, this
thorax, red into violet. Berry-

pick a way past nakedhood
you're sure to miss the alphabet
for which our babies plead and
chirally kiss. Out of the field

office and into the fescue, out
of the forage grass and into
the field, out of the fire and
into the fallow, that is, if

we plan to go night clear. Bring
new salts, berries, warped
wingback, paisley tears: Our
observation has sped up how

terminal each rosette, yet
sadness, will it go? Fast,
slow, like water on pavement,
pennies in politics, like blame

on education, fangled ego
in horizontal vision, flocculent
like shame on small children,
molluskan, bullets in desperation,

drones not aimed at civilians,
like mauvish bromides in rivers
flow to every crack along young
muds, freeze, break apart and go

to that rocky place, or sweet
evaporate, be, no truck,
a dewsome thing we watch like
"Please come where I can see."

DELTA DAWN FORCE

Stars no more
my commitment
equipment
now than when
your schedule calls
truce with one
nearly decent hour
to hush, mere as
the money some
paper over vibrancy
with. Stars
are crucial
shrapnel, cutting
clear through
the wallow
to invite you
into your own
fluency: a few
rosy frills
around elision,
not the sort
that omits, sort of
just running

together, fast
and for survival,
where I can go
to be smoothed
across rocks
like butter.

TENDERSHIP

Enjoy the juice
loose in the jar
with plausible buoy
that may be reversed
robust and natal to
fast movings
off-center. Each
slip down my gullet
your calyx
commemorates tender
ships astray
from their ports
—the dominant
festers, the dormant
fosters; the dominant
fastens, the dormant
fascinates.

SIGN

Tremble gone
unnoticed till
a familiar pen
gets in your hand.
Anything held
starts to tell
how we move.

TARNATION ENCYCLICAL

I have to plant this
how it reels, the year
so young with dread
and old, over a little
lettuce bed. Over and
over, again it nipples
another suck to water
while what I want
is corn higher
than the waves
that are coming
and none of it, the corn,
heading into
our cars. The root
of my feeling calls
me to feel for
the root, building up
each stressful cataphyll
the parenthetical
texture of fellowship
and readably as
curled, daring to be
dear to me. Even a trace

of belonging
glitters through—like voice,
lament the kind
of contraption
you could say
merely holding
teaches us to use. Henbit
preempts the moon
its decision to apply
such squalling moral
talents, mauve, across
an octave, operative
and baroque. Together
we roast how coffee
courts the thunderhead
before watering
the plants. I too
water the plants,
which makes me feel
good. Oh, good,
another feeling
to interrogate.

TAGELIED

After hearts
what breaks
that isolation
rattles
my starlet
concentration
like breath
in the first
cool stages
of relief
shakes fey
outfits—their
impossible knit
and sessile
blush—from
springtime. Because
the minimal grove
that is
our health
sprigs off
in every
direction, I can feel
its fatal interview

coming on
in a practical
strewment
of what wants
to save the world
except the world.

DISTRACTING INJURY

I will not be unwithered.
Celebration
with its scalloped edges
pulls everything
in close, so
there's no hour
not your birthday
in my heart, while
a modern fondness
for worship might be
the nonviolent wallop
of one's constant,
frantic stomach.

NONCE HEX FOR "ROMANTIC LOVE, THE LAST ILLUSION," WHICH WILL "[KEEP] US ALIVE UNTIL THE REVOLUTIONS COME"

Laughing hard
as the bones
inside a mountain,
baffled by the blank
flowers flooding
her alps with therapy,
a claw washes through
in gashes the sky
a credible pamphlet
brown amounting
to fog. But hardly
wrenched, was it
joy? Your moan
I try to follow
by some college-ruled
light—how much
we try to hold
up to vibrancy
for protection: Though
we may never know
how to go

on when it comes, that
cumulative song,
which nets first and last
quite the very tops
of trees, let us be
caught, not always
off guard.

NOTES

"Conspicuous pang" – a take on the Emily Dickinson line "A Pang is more conspicuous in Spring"

"you be ardent" – from a poem by Sappho translated by A.S. Kline

"You and I fall together. You and I sleep alone." and "All you're ever losing..." – from "Little Mascara" by The Replacements

"Impromptu baby" – from "Take Me or Leave Me" from *Rent* by Jonathan Larson

"But, Jimmy, he talks just as sweet as you." – from "Jimmy Mack" by Lamont Dozier, Brian Holland and Eddie Holland

"It's just a flower made out of clay... it's hard to live in the city." – from "Ride into the Sun" by Lou Reed

"Please come where I can see." – from "J" by Ani DiFranco

"fatal interview" – from the title of a sonnet collection by Edna St. Vincent Millay

"Romantic love, the last illusion, keeps us alive until the revolutions come." – from *The Faggots & Their Friends Between Revolutions* by Larry Mitchell

"Livingry" – a term credited to R. Buckminster Fuller; the opposite of "weaponry," or "killingry"

ACKNOWLEDGMENTS

I am thankful to Ben Lerner, Jamie Townsend, Nicholas DeBoer, and Connie Mae Oliver for homing earlier versions of several of these poems with *Critical Quarterly*, *Elderly*, and *Feelings*.

I am also deeply indebted to MC Hyland, Anna Gurton-Wachter, and Jeff Peterson for their great care and sensitive labor in publishing "Catena" as a chapbook with DoubleCross Press.

During impossible periods of trying self-doubt, exchanges with these poets and editors refreshed, refleshed and reflooded.

For the above and so many other reasons am I grateful, infinitely, for the hearts, minds, and hands of Stephen Motika, Lindsey Boldt, Andrea Abi-Karam, Shelby Hettler, HR Hegnauer, and the whole Nightboat crew—their being truly inimitable in the ways of wisdom, encouragement, guidance, patience, and passion.

•   •   •

The bulk of this book came to me in St. Louis; my praise goes to the rich writing community there, which, knowing or not, held me together. Justin Phillip Reed, thank you for the Most Folks workshop, and thank you to workshop members Susan Trowbridge Adams, Pacia Anderson,

Joss Barton, Shine Goodie, and Alison C. Rollins. For discussions of contemporary poetry, for food, drink and camaraderie, my sincere appreciation goes to Rachel Greenwald Smith, Ted Mathys, Christopher Miller, Jessica Baran, Nathaniel Farrell, Jeff Hamilton, and Devin Johnston. Bhanu Kapil, thank you for the workshop component of your project "How to Grieve and Dream at the Same Time"; Philip Matthews and Aaron Coleman, thank you for making it happen; and thank you to all the workshop members—those already named above as well as Baba Badji, Jason Kei, Maura Pellettieri, Treasure Shields Redmond, Niel Rosenthalis, Stephanie Ellis Schlaifer, Sahara Sista SOLS Scott, and Freeman Word.

•   •   •

The bulk of this book is owed to Willis, whom I know in a way that creeps toward forever, and Harken, our darling I've only just met.

NIGHTBOAT BOOKS

Nightboat Books, a nonprofit organization, seeks to develop audiences for writers whose work resists convention and transcends boundaries. We publish books rich with poignancy, intelligence, and risk. Please visit our website, www.nightboat.org, to learn about our titles and how you can support our future publications.

The following individuals have supported the publication of this book. We thank them for their generosity and commitment to the mission of Nightboat Books:

Kazim Ali
Anonymous
Photios Giovanis
Elenor & Thomas Kovachevich
Elizabeth Motika
Leslie Scalapino – O Books Fund
Benjamin Taylor
Jerrie Whitfield & Richard Motika

In addition, this book has been made possible, in part, by grants from the National Endowment for the Arts and New York State Council on the Arts Literature Program.